Publishing Credits

Dona Herweck Rice, *Editor-in-Chief*
Lee Aucoin, *Creative Director*
Kristy Stark, M.A.Ed., *Senior Editor*
Torrey Maloof, *Editor*
Kristine Magnien, M.S.Ed., *Associate Education Editor*
Neri Garcia, *Senior Designer*
Stephanie Reid, *Photo Researcher*
Rachelle Cracchiolo, M.S.Ed., *Publisher*

Image Credits

cover: Thinkstock; pp. 1,3,14,18,20,33,35,37,38 iStockphoto; all other images from Shutterstock.

Teacher Created Materials
5301 Oceanus Drive
Huntington Beach, CA 92649-1030
http://www.tcmpub.com
ISBN 978-1-4333-4781-8
©2013 Teacher Created Materials, Inc.
Made in China
Nordica.072017.CA21700826

Table of Contents

Dear Family,

Congratulations! You've wisely enrolled your child in school to help prepare him or her for kindergarten. Your child may have been in day care and is familiar with organized activities. Or, this may be the first time that your child has been away from home for an extended period of time. While some children take a while to adjust to a school setting, there is one thing true about most youngsters at this age—they love learning!

There are many changes ahead, but there is one other constant besides this natural love of learning; you will continue to be the most important teacher in your child's life. This parent guide will give you some ideas for continuing this role of helping your child learn, from tips for getting organized, to learning on the go throughout your busy day. Some of these practices will be familiar and some will be new. Many will serve you well for the next dozen or more years!

One last thought...

Your child's teacher can be a great resource, so stay in touch and know that questions are welcome!

A Great
Start

Remember when you could get organized during your child's afternoon naps? Those days are either already gone or will be in the very near future! And, if you work outside the home as well, getting organized is even more important. Here's the good news...your child can help!

Try these ideas to help your child be organized and responsible.

In- and Out-Boxes

Establish a time to go through the papers your child brings home. If you arrive home after your prekindergartner does, have an in-box for your child. Review the materials, and those that go back to the school can be put in an out-box.

Chores

Take time to establish age-appropriate chores and responsibilities with your child.

School at Home

Keep a regular time of 15 to 20 minutes for reading or looking at picture books.

One last thought...

Maintain a regular "work" schedule
for your child so that a routine
is established.

Listen
Up!

Your prekindergartner is learning to listen attentively. Create daily routines that will help your child focus and develop his or her attention span.

Try these activities that combine learning with working out the wiggles.

Go Fish

Create a set of cards with about 15 letter or number matches. Deal out four cards for each. Player 1 asks, "Do you have a card with the letter A?" If so, player 2 gives up the card, and player 1 puts down the pair. If not, player 1 draws a card from the deck until he or she has a pair. The game ends when there are no cards left!

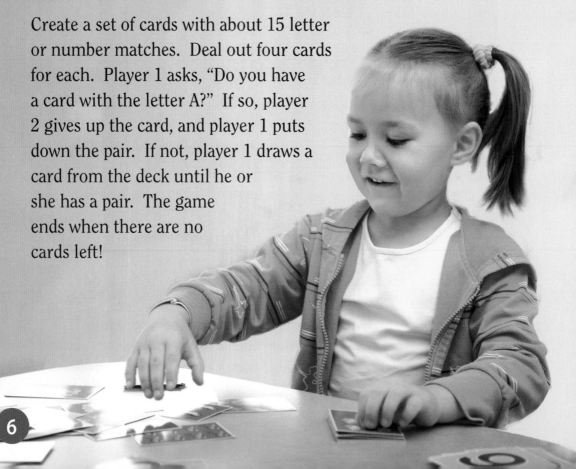

Simon Says

Simon Says is a great way for children to practice his or her learning skills. Add variations to the game by changing the name of the game. *Grandma Says* can be a fun twist on a familiar game.

Patterns

Create a sound and movement pattern for your child to repeat, such as clap-clap, stomp-stomp, clap-stomp-clap-stomp.

One last thought...

Use simple games when you are in the car, such as saying, "I'm going to say three words. You tell me which one starts with a different sound: *cat, cow, ball.*"

Talk It Up!

For most parents, the first few words uttered by their child were magical. Before long, those single words turned into sentences and even paragraphs! Your child's vocabulary is still growing, and conversations are a great way to continue vocabulary development.

Try some of these ideas to help build vocabulary.

Story Picture

Glue about 20 pictures on 5 x 7 inch index cards: animals, people, houses, objects, toys, plants, etc. Deal into four stacks, face down. Have your child turn over the top cards and make up a story. Take turns.

Guess Where

Give your child a small object, such as a button or ball, to hide while you leave the room. When you return, your child should give one clue at a time to help you find the object.
Then, trade roles.

Guess My Picture

Place pictures in a box or bag. Have your child choose a picture at random and describe it without saying its name, such as, "This has stripes." The other players try to guess what the picture is. After three guesses, another clue is added, such as, "It purrs."

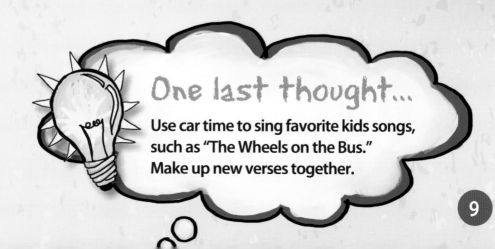

One last thought...

Use car time to sing favorite kids songs, such as "The Wheels on the Bus." Make up new verses together.

Sleep
Is Good for You!

If your prekindergartner has not been around lots of other children, prepare yourself for exposure to a few more rounds of sniffles this year. Having an early bedtime so your child gets enough sleep is crucial to your child's health.

The chart below shows how much sleep children need.

Age	Sleep Needed
1–3 years	12–14 hours
3–5 years	11–13 hours
5–12 years	10–11 hours

These tips will help your prekindergartner get enough sleep:

Routine

Create a routine with the same bedtime, lighting, and temperature each night.

Be Prepared

Make setting out the next day's clothes part of your child's nightly routine.

Quiet Time

Make it a relaxing time without TV or videos.

Read Aloud

Read aloud a favorite picture book.

One last thought...

If your child has persistent sleep issues or night terrors, have a chat with your pediatrician.

Top 10
Things Your Prekindergartner
Needs to Know

1. How to listen to a **read-aloud** by the teacher

2. How to **ask** and **answer** questions about a story or book

3. **That written words** correspond to **spoken words**

4. Reading from **left to right** and from the **top to the bottom** of the page

5. **Singing and reciting** songs and poems

6. Learning about **numbers** by counting objects

7. Practicing **making shapes**

8. Comparing **height** and **weight**

9. Recognizing **color** and **size** patterns

10. **Sorting objects** by color, size, and shape

13

Vocabulary
Building Blocks

Parents serve as role models for their children's vocabulary. It is important to use adult vocabulary when talking with your child, and explain new vocabulary words as they arise. This is the best way to learn new words!

Try some of these activities
to build vocabulary.

Paper Chain

Make a paper chain together, writing all the words your child and you can think of in a category such as animal babies, colors, number words, fruits, toys, names of shapes, etc.

Rhyming Words

Have fun with rhyming words. Start with an animal and think of an item that rhymes, such as a goat in a boat. Draw pictures for each other and guess the rhymes.

Labels

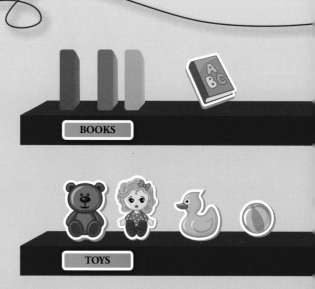

Label closets, objects in the room, categories of toys, book shelves, etc. Give your child the responsibility of putting things away according to labels.

Games

Play a variation of "Duck, Duck, Goose" by choosing a category, such as vehicles. "It" walks around the circle, touching each player in turn, saying something like "bike, car, van, truck," eventually using a non-vehicle word, such as "pizza." At that point, the pizza designee gets up, chasing "It" around to the vacated seat. The one who did the chasing becomes "It."

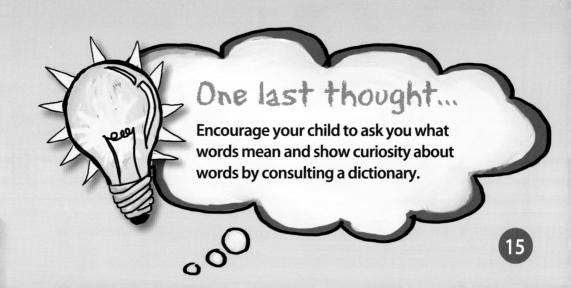

One last thought...

Encourage your child to ask you what words mean and show curiosity about words by consulting a dictionary.

A Print
Rich Environment

Your prekindergartner probably already reads many words. Some words may have been learned at school and others from the world around them. Many children can recognize their favorite store names and other common signs.

Capitalize on learning new words with these ideas when you are out in the community.

Traffic Signs

Read the various traffic signs as you approach them. If your child is still learning the letters of the alphabet, ask him or her to identify the first letter of a sign and its sound.

Bilingual Signs

Use bilingual signs to reinforce two languages. Have your child read words, such as exit, push, pull, etc.

SPEED LIMIT 50

RADAR ENFORCED

WRONG WAY

Food Labels

Have your child fetch the correct can of food from your pantry or save the labels from food cans and boxes. Have your child practice reading them.

Maps

Show the utility of print by reading and using maps in malls, transportation centers, etc.

One last thought...

Reading environmental print —or the print in the world around us—shows that your child is already a reader!

Phonics
Play

Every time you read aloud or talk about letters and words, you are laying the foundation for phonics instruction. Learning letters and sounds will help your child become a successful reader.

Here are some ideas to develop your child's phonemic awareness.

Ask

Ask your prekindergartner to cut out pictures in junk mail, toy catalogs, or sales fliers. Have him or her sort them into piles with words that start with the same sounds.

Blend

Blend routine activities with phonics play. Start by saying, "Put on something that begins with the same sound as sand." (Answer: socks.) You can make this more challenging over time by using ending or middle (vowel) sounds.

Create

Create an alphabet book on a specific theme, such as animals, insects, vehicles, toys, etc. Label each page: A Words, B Words, etc. Find or draw pictures that match each letter to fill the pages.

Develop

Find pictures of objects from A to Z and glue them separately on 3 x 5 inch cards. Write each letter of the alphabet on a separate stack of cards. Choose 5 matching letters and pictures of objects, mix them up, and lay them face down. Turn over pairs, matching the letter with the picture of the object. Make this concentration game more challenging by increasing the number of cards used.

One last thought...

Be alert to opportunities to point out wordplay, such as tongue twisters: *Peter Piper picked a peck of pickled peppers*....

Book
Picks

Thousands of picture books are published each year. Ask your librarian for lists of award-winning books, such as those that have won the Caldecott Medal for outstanding illustrations.

Here are some books your child might enjoy.

- *The Very Hungry Caterpillar* by Eric Carle
- *Olivia* by Ian Falconer
- *Singing-Time* by Rose Fyleman
- *Celebration* by Alonzo Lopez
- *Alphabatics* by Sue MacDonald
- *Goldilocks and the Three Bears* by James Marshall
- *Chicka Chicka Boom Boom* by Bill Martin Jr.
- *The Kindergarten Diary* by Antoinette Portis
- *No, David!* by David Shannon
- *Knuffle Bunny Too: A Case of Mistaken Identity* by Mo Willems

One last thought...

Read aloud a variety of books to your child. Read with humor and expression!

Print
At Home

Prekindergartners are developing their literacy skills. They are learning to connect oral and written language. Expose your child to pictures, books, and magazines to help him or her understand that important connection.

Here are some fun ideas for you to do at home!

1. **Read aloud** to your child every day. Talk about what you read.

2. Let your child **see you reading** for pleasure and for information.

3. Give your child paper and crayons and let him or her **use invented spelling.**

4. Get your child a **library card** and use it frequently.

5. **Point out signs** on the bus, on the street, at the market, etc., and read them together.

FRUITS

VEGGIES

Math
Starts

If you offer to cut your prekindergartner's sandwiches into triangles, you've been teaching geometry. You are teaching one-to-one correspondence each time you say, "Take two more bites. One…two."

These activities will help you reinforce math concepts on-the-go.

Traffic Signs

Almost any shape can be taught with traffic signs. As you drive or ride the bus, make a game of finding all the triangles, octagons, etc. You can reinforce colors, as well.

License Plates

Have your child find numbers on license plates, starting with number one.

Counting Songs

Sing counting songs to your child, such as "Six Little Ducks" or "The Ants Go Marching." You can find lyrics for these and dozens of kids' songs at http://kids.niehs.nih.gov/.

123 ABC

Market Math

The grocery store is a perfect place to reinforce math. Count the cans of soup you're buying. Have your child find the heaviest pumpkin. Have him or her identify numbers in prices, weights, and product codes.

One last thought...

It's tempting to race through chores. Slow down and take the time to involve your child in the process. Children are eager to help at this age!

Math
In Action

Does your child pour water from one container to another during bath time? Compare his or her height to a sibling? Complain when a sibling has a larger cookie? That's math in action.

• •

Encourage active math with these fun activities.

Educational Play

Combine play with counting and other mathematical concepts. This can be done by counting cars while driving or singing counting songs.

Pretend Market

When you come home from the store, have your prekindergartner sort and put away the cans. Save your clean, empty cans and food boxes and let your child set up a grocery store. Encourage him or her to make pretend money for purchases.

Math Books

Let books with a math theme inspire activities in the house, such as counting out items while setting the table. *Goldilocks and the Three Bears* includes sizing, counting, and comparison. See your library for ideas, such as *Roll Over* by Merle Peek and *One Monkey Too Many* by Jackie French Koller.

Sorting and Classifying

Ever wondered what to do with all those extra buttons you'll never need? Put them in a box for your prekindergartner to sort by color, size, design, and material.

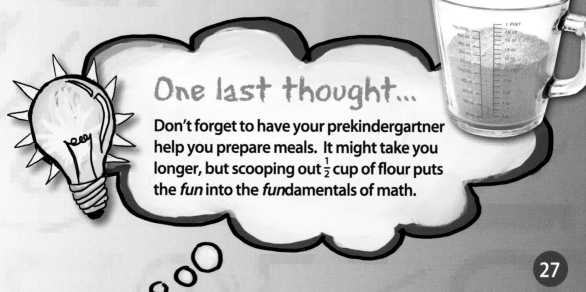

One last thought...

Don't forget to have your prekindergartner help you prepare meals. It might take you longer, but scooping out $\frac{1}{2}$ cup of flour puts the *fun* into the *fun*damentals of math.

Math
At Home

Prekindergartners are exploring the world around them. They are discovering math as they sort, classify, compare quantities, balance blocks, and find shapes and patterns. Helping at home is an easy way for your child to build his or her math skills!

Bring math into your home with some of these fun tips.

Cook with your Child

Involve your child in measuring ingredients when you cook. When you are finished, enjoy your meal or snack together!

Play Money

Turn your cupboard into a pretend market. Let your child shop in the cupboard and use coins or make pretend money to buy each item.

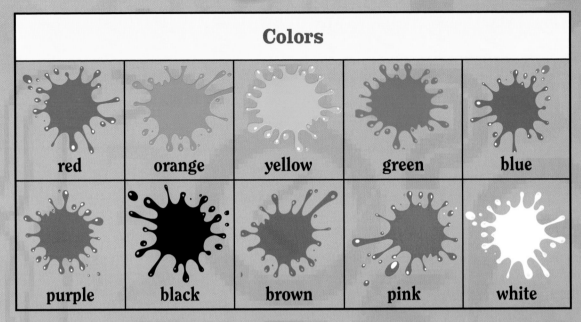

Colors				
red	orange	yellow	green	blue
purple	black	brown	pink	white

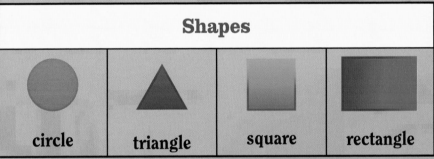

Shapes			
circle	triangle	square	rectangle

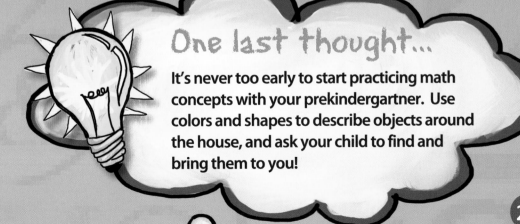

One last thought...

It's never too early to start practicing math concepts with your prekindergartner. Use colors and shapes to describe objects around the house, and ask your child to find and bring them to you!

Natural
Science

Young children are naturally curious. Take advantage of this curiosity and go outside together to explore nature.

Encourage your child's natural interest in science with these activities.

Listen

Walk to a favorite spot and sit quietly. Record the sounds in a journal, from insects to passing vehicles. Use both pictures and words in the journal.

Observe

What happens when you add food coloring to water, oil, milk, liquid detergent, or a combination of the liquids? Or, when you leave a small piece of ripe fruit on a plate for several days?

Collect

Collect rocks, leaves, soil, flowers, and insects. Talk about how things are the same and how they are different.

Explore

Gather a variety of objects, such as light and heavy paper, white and colored paper, clear and colored glass bottles, etc. What happens when they are placed in the sun?

Touch

Touch and describe things that are smooth and rough, soft and hard, and round and flat.

Journal

Use an appointment notebook to record discoveries while reinforcing the names of the days of the week and changes in the environment over time.

One last thought...

Some discoveries are totally unplanned. So, be prepared to take extra time to enjoy those unexpected investigations.

The Social
World

Prekindergartners have learned that their social network is more than their immediate family. They are fascinated with the people, such as community workers, whom they observe or encounter.

Encourage a deeper understanding of people and their roles with these activities.

Big Trucks

Do you know the difference between a backhoe and a front end loader? It's time to learn! Many children are fascinated with heavy equipment and the building process. Read the classic *Mike Mulligan and His Steam Shovel* by Virginia Lee Burton.

Community Jobs

Talk about the workers in the community and how they help others. Police officers keep us safe, doctors help when we are sick, and postal workers deliver our mail. Encourage your child to dress up and pretend play as these community workers.

Scrapbook

Create a scrapbook together that documents special days, outings, family events, and celebrations. Include unique family traditions.

Cultural Celebrations

Ask an older family member or neighbor to prepare traditional food. Introduce one new ethnic food a month to your family. If ethnic food is already part of your child's life, talk about why this type of food is important to your family.

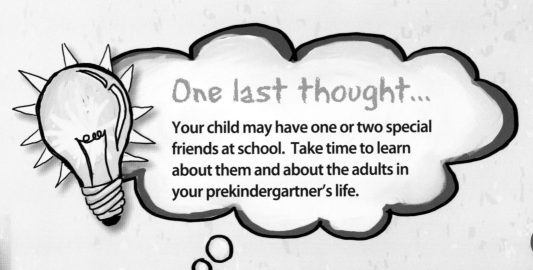

One last thought...

Your child may have one or two special friends at school. Take time to learn about them and about the adults in your prekindergartner's life.

33

Beyond School

Many prekindergartners still benefit from an afternoon nap. Others have lots of energy and are already developing specific interests. Talk with your child and consider choosing after-school activities.

Try some of these fun after-school activities.

Science
Check with the science museum, children's museum, or zoo for classes that investigate science.

Sports
Your recreation center, sports centers, YWCA, or YMCA may offer ballet, swimming lessons, gymnastics, and a variety of sports. Your child may want to try several choices before settling on his or her favorite.

Music
Look for classes at art or music centers that explore singing, making instruments, and rhythmic movement.

Art
Check with the recreation centers, children's museums, and libraries for classes that explore art.

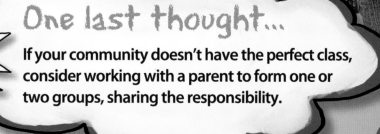

One last thought...
If your community doesn't have the perfect class, consider working with a parent to form one or two groups, sharing the responsibility.

Learning
To Go

Learning can happen anywhere. Take advantage of your time spent outside of the home and turn it into learning opportunities for your child.

Use these activities to build your child's knowledge.

Counting

Have your child count as you drive: animals, white vans, people on bikes, squares, stop signs.

A-Z

Write the letters from A to Z on a sheet of paper. Put it on a clipboard with a pencil attached. As you drive along, have your child look for things that start with the letters, such as *c* for *cow*, checking off the corresponding letter.

Favorites

Play the Favorites game. Begin by asking each person in the car to identify his or her favorite color. Pass the turn to another to ask for a favorite video game, board game, ice cream flavor, book, movie, etc.

One last thought...

When your child gets tired while riding, put on soothing music or an audio book.

Keep
Playing!

Ralph Waldo Emerson once said, "It is a happy talent to know how to play." Luckily for us parents—we get to keep playing with our kids.

• •

Try some of these group games with family and friends to keep the fun going.

Bumper Tag

Play a fun game of Bumper Tag with your family. The person who is "It" tags or bumps others gently with his or her hips. Be sure to remind your child that no one should be knocked over with his or her hip bump!

Hug Tag

For Hug Tag, you can stay "safe" by hugging someone else for a count of five seconds.

Tunnel Tag

To play Tunnel Tag, find a spot where there's a fence or wall. Once tagged, the players must stand two feet or so from the wall, with one arm stretched out to the wall. An untagged player can set them free by running under the outstretched arm. The game ends when everyone has been caught at least once.

Fruit Basket Upset

To play Fruit Basket Upset, choose three or more fruit names. Assign fruit names to players by counting off, such as apple, pear, banana, apple, pear, etc. Have a circle of chairs for all but one of the players. "It" calls out the name of a fruit, and the players assigned to that fruit change spots. When "It" calls "fruit basket upset," everyone races to a chair, including the leader. The person who is without a seat becomes "It."

One last thought...

Keep the focus on having fun, not on winning or losing.

Dear Parent,

You have a great year ahead! Your prekindergartner will be learning so much, and you'll be learning, too. Thank you for squeezing in some time to read this booklet. We hope that it gave you a few ideas for making the year even better.

Remember to stay in touch with your child's teacher and other adults that interact with him or her each day. Everyone wants the same thing—to ensure that your child is ready for that next big milestone—kindergarten! Believe it or not, it's right around the corner.

Thank you!